ON THE LEDGE

RIFKA KRUMMEL

ISBN: 978-0-9963433-3-6
Library of Congress Control Number: 2017936824

Published in the United States by Wasabi Cat Publishing,
Tacoma, WA 98407
www.wasabicat.com

To all our children in a world of peace.
For Yetta, Shoshana, Amita, Maya, Phoebe
and Apollo.

And the Gates Clang Shut

"They let us out to kick a ball, smoke our lungs out, mop the toilets and floors, shove us back and the gates clang shut." Rikers Island student, prisoner, She wonders as she gets her hand stamped about the rehabilitation in this locked away environment. Julio writes, "Got a new racist asshole in the lower bunk He is a vicious cursing angry dude full of venom. This is the worst of the detention centers I've been in. Nothing to do but figure out how to destroy each other. One must never seem vulnerable or scared. If you seem like a victim you're dead meat."

They write of their lives - past, present, no future. The Fox writes, "I want to break every one of the rules. All we get is don't do anything. Nothing is positive. I got hit with a broom for not cleaning well."

I get in, get out and try to dig myself out of the abyss.

Bazooka

Serious talk
"Cellmate took a rope
Tied himself
Jumped up

Not dead
Just a mess
Screw done
Dragged him out
By his arms

Slapped alive
Not my cellmate
No more."

The cell door
Has eye view
Window
Outside Block A

"It's full of ghosts, Regina
Guys died here
Block A
Full of dead thoughts
Lifeless feelings

My granddad
Strong, big, lover of life
He left the world
Slopping up baby food

Granddad
Died
No, couldn't go
He wasn't no
Mum or Dad

Never seen him again
I'm here
He's dead
Over

Wow, Regina
You got Bazooka gum
I won't chew it
I'll keep It."

Why didn't I bring a dozen boxes
Of bubble gum
Chew our words
Read poetry

Eat words with sugar
Our love,
Our world
Together.

"Stray Bullet Kills Boy, 2, in Bronx"
- The New York Times, Monday, April 19, 2006

Bronx Boy

Like a rag doll
Blood ran
From his body

Killed in a car
Bullets missed their mark
Baby killed

Settling a gang score
Perhaps many disputes

Bronx moments
Continues...
Baby unknown to warring groups
Housing projects and tenements
Far from Darfur, Iran, Iraq, Haiti
Deep in a lovely dream
In his padded seat

Waiting to begin a life
As Frost knew "Nothing to build on..."
The baby was always smiling
Neighbors agreed

He was so loved.
He always laughed.

Calm

Calm…no tempest

Conversation so warm
Ingratiating

"We are such stuff
As dreams are made of…
What strength I have is mine own
Which is most faint.
Set me free…"
Shakespeare's theme
Unfulfilled
His last known play.

We chat about wars
Prisons
Crimes, humiliations
Traded in lockup
Guards and victims

So clear, civil, kind
We do not worship
Asses, fools, drunks
We seek calm seas, gentle breezes
Our paths are clear
Skies are blue.

"Do not go where the path may lead, go where there
is no path."   - Emerson
"I have taken the road less traveled. That has made
all the difference."   - Frost

China

Why did we decide on China?

We met Chinese teachers
Some silent, shy
Eyes cast down

The heat was oppressive
We changed our cotton outfits
Twice a day.

Pavements bleached, in the broken crevices
Baby excrement

Men huddled around stoves
Cooking rice and ribs.

Roads congested
With animals, cabs and bikes
Blasting horns and screaming people.

Did I find myself in paradise?
Singing of hope and planted trees
Happy children?
No envy, hate, rivalry.

I am sealed in the sound
Of expectation.

Clasping Hands

We clasp our hands in a frenzy of togetherness
A fleeting gesture
Followed by isolation and aloneness
I am the fool in the opera.
So I persist and moan.

I fear the frozen road of letting go.
It is humiliating and degrading
As one who is a card carrying professor
Do I know who I am?
We are all ash
But I must persist
No God will shelter me

Cry

Cry…cry baby

Weeping minstrel
Hot sweats
Nails lacerated
I sit in car
Can't drive away
Ignition key
In my clenched fist.

Push the hazard panel
Pulsating, bleating cow
Sounds…flashing, flashing
Head bent over wheel

Can't stay
Must stay
"Cry baby…cry baby."

Forever…
Forever?

December

It is December

We compose
Our lives
From the shards of troubled pasts
Lies, subterfuge, escape
"Let's Pretend" childhood games of mangled dreams
Fears, destruction
Cloaked in pristine behavior
Smiling at cameras
In a long series of performances
Father - mothers
History
We search for a speck of hope
A moment of discovery.

Desultory

Decrepit, desultory, indolent
Cancer moves underground
Silently observing, unnoticed
Daily events
Food, wealth, beauty treatments
Cars
Flooded highways
Oh well.

Cells do their thing
Lazy, forceful, meandering actively
In a decisive dance
Of death.

We wait
Struggle

Seek logical
Answers
Enter a jumbled heap
As armies clash in daylight.

"The speech we hear is an indication of that which we don't hear. It is a necessary avoidance, a violent slip, anguished or mocking smoke screen which keeps the other in place."

- Harold Pinter, playwright

Do We Hear?

Do we hear?

Are we dying
For the living?
Are we laughing
For the sorrow?
Are we hugging
For the loneliness?

Eradicating our innards
Our hopes
Our memories
Our actions
Our desires
Our passions?

Are we living
For the joy
Of living?

Dr. K

Hey, Dr. K., it's been a long, long story
Back to my granma
To her granma

We got some angry men
In our lives
We was from a large body tribe
We was big, black, boisterous
We yelled when happy and sad

No get away from smooth talking men

Got me enough kids
Leave me be
Keep your dick inside.
No more kids.

No more cookin,' cleanin,' nursin'
Everybody's baby

It's enough for five lives
It is enough.

Dropping the Ball

Yeah, once again the ball was dropped
I saw it on TV
I did not drop the ball
Neither did the Cuban boy
Stolen from his life
He went home to his father who knew his shoe size
Became an adult.

That ball
Has no balls
Numerous or few
It's not an empty womb
A tomb or a ball to kick
Or throw.
It celebrates
Many perfumes, under garments
Shaving lotions, wrinkle curing creams and moisturizers
On this New Year always be happy
And blow on the noise maker.

Empty Courts

So quiet
Empty, deflated
Struggle seems
Trifling
Talking heads and toes
And everything in between
All know the value of things
Yes, value
Ask Yahoo
Ask Facebook
The value of friendship
Or actually listening
Actually touching
Actually sharing
In death we do part.

Events

Events pile haphazardly
Across days
Sludge and slime
Stealthily creeping
Infecting bodies
Destroying feelings of love
Of devotion

Grasping, holding on
Joints twisted, painful
Gnarled fingers
Crushed hopes

Meaning?

We grapple with power
Controlled by perfected
Denial

Frozen smiles
Fixed, stagnant patterns
Behavior
Noisy buzz
Promising
What?

"...exploit every weakness, demolish every initiative, negate all signs of individuality—all with the idea of stamping out that spark that makes each of us human and each of us who we are."

- Nelson Mandela

Exploit Every Weakness

I heard this from the pregnant young woman, Shandra, shut off from personal responsibility or becoming an adult. She whined while waiting for sentencing on drug possession and, of course, her own addiction gave her the illusion to go on. Two million people are in prison and the number grows. Drug users continue to be incarcerated.

We have a prison era. Kids born into poverty and hopelessness turn to the huge culture of drugs costing people hundreds of billions a year.

Prison is a harsh reality. Who is inside? Who experiences sadistic control? Who bangs their heads against walls?

She wonders about her own habits. The poor, the mentally ill are warehoused in prisons. They are kept in cells the size of bathrooms. "My Mom was in prison when I was born," Dwayne tells me. "I lived with my grandma who told me to shut up because I cried every night. I ran away from my grandma's house every few weeks and wandered around the Chicago slum we lived in. I tried to kill myself when I was ten. I swallowed rat poison, but I got so sick I ended up in the hospital with a punctured abdomen wall. I was sent to a juvenile home for disturbed youth. My mom got fifteen years for cocaine possession. She's rotting in prison like me." He was sobbing and unable to talk.

He did return to the group but never spoke again. Finally he said, "I really want new sneakers." Brands are special when worn by great athletes. Money pours in and kids like Dwayne just want those fashionable brands worn by their idols. Clothes, shoes, cars, sunglasses, drugs, smokes—all in the plan. Going where?

Fear of People

I do not fear people and spaces
Open or closed.
I fear sadists and betrayers
Who scream their truths
Lock others in
Suffering poverty of spirit

We throw away our victims
Like mounds of salt piles
Landfill garbage
We write pads of RX drugs
Silence the voices
Their endless monotony
Relentlessly surviving
Exile, isolation
Closed boxes
Airless futures
Throw-away ads.

Fluids

Plural? Singular? The world as we individuals experience it. Old age is packed with concern for hydration, no place for little dried up old crones. Yes? Who cares? Drink while our water still comes; the neglected earth grows more scary, more frightening. Who knows how our oligarchs view the pleasure stream of spas and steam baths and bubble surfaces that seize their momentary pleasure needs in the fluid pool of our world.

The rant now completed, she thinks. What about her sisters in cell blocks moving in shackles and wrist cuffs lined up to be "escorted" into the room for poetry discussion? Poetry? Life? Fluid drained from body, dead sex, no spirit, just anger moans and dies. Bubbling pool, great whiskey, scintillating conversation... How was the buffalo burger? Too dry...

Waiting for the end. Virginia Woolf secures stones and places them in her coat pockets and decides to walk into the water, the ultimate life fluid, drowning in the maternal sac, letting go, frenzy of wetness, absence of climax, final denouement... all fluid. Urination as the final emptying and nothingness.

Fluid needs are replete with problems. In India the schools for the Dalit, the poor, require toilets with separate pits for boys and girls. Perhaps we should continue to empty ourselves in the thousands of years of garbage and debris? The debate continues and involves police, government consultants, plumbing experts and various gurus. Where to pee? On highways, behind gated communities, at dead seas like Salton Sea in California, on the collection of human waste and garbage all over our globe. By the waters of Babylon, Hudson, Gowanus Canal, East River, Long Island Sound, the Ganges, all strewn with life debris of plastic, chemicals, needles, fecal matter. We occupy and leave behind crap. Fluids in sewers becomes tourist destinations to observe dripping on cave walls.

We played in the city streets growing up and imagined a different life in a mythic village of flowing fountains, streams, lovely lakes and waterways. When the bad boys taunted us, we rolled the saliva in our mouths, gathered the spit and spat the contempt with the fluid. Spitting is not acceptable for little ladies, the teacher announced, but the flow of wetness hit the mark.

Don't you think you should have some delicious water? After all, every spring is utilized to market and bottle elegance in health food shops. Perhaps bottled herbal fluid from the bodies of young athletes is a significant dietary delight as yet unexplored as an added complement to hydration in a self-actualization regimen. I suggest a deep blue bottle for this special liquid.

Fluid is so needed for our athletic prowess that all types of drinking paraphernalia must be enlisted—plastic (recyclable), steel, ceramic, paper. We need tasters who sip and report and those who "settle" for availability.

No bottled water for prisoners. Guards, therapists, drink sodas and bottled water while prisoners squirm in shackles and fart. So hot here. I want to go to my cell and sleep. Just wait. Lunch is on the way. Line up, don't shove, don't ask for water. To ask is to be brutalized. Curse, don't spit, stay steady, always alert, drink nothing from a sink might be contaminated - rusty pipes, get sicker and wait. Who knows? Sorry I have no choice, medical doctors. They're all doing it. It? Yes…The life fluids drain out. The horror is abuse, boredom, clanging metal, screaming. No water. Cell blocks with rusty sink. "Lights out now." Choice? Submission or beating. A toilet, a sink, a miniature world with no release, no stimulation, endless dry, devastating days.

No cold, white wine on a humid, hot day, no cold coffee for afternoon break just mop the floor, clean the crap, two showers a week in dirty stalls. I need a hot water bottle for my aching head. Nothing. I used to wash my hair four times a week. Nothing now, shut up. I used to dance, drink, walk freely. I think I did. No right to shower when I want to. All body parts regulated. Urinate into bottle, search for drugs. Degrade, humiliate, female body not your own, rape at will. Don't complain.

And then the tears flow. Yes, human fluid reflecting the horror of nurturing servility, passivity, knee bending pretense in the "best of all possible worlds." The frustration of viewing violence while remaining stoic, accepting the banality of evil (Hannah Arendt). The self-indulgent sobbing is so comforting, better than s death swim. "Pull yourself together" you mutter. Eyeless in Gaza, are you? The broken bodies lying in piles amid bombed houses. The luxury of weeping, dripping eyes, nose, mouth. "She cares," phrase of missionary pleasure. Weep on to reveal the deeply caring woman, a martyr at last.

Think I need to swim out/on. Can't. Water envelops my body, releases my breath, too long, too much...water, weeping, coming, yes, release, no more begging. Remembering succulent fruit, mango, papaya, flowing into my mouth, rain on a hot day, wet desire and quenched thirst.

Half Empty, Half Full

Glass...half empty, half full?

What do I see?
Inside
It is both
Conflicts, victim of marketing
"Sold a bill of goods..."

I walk the track
I swing my arms
I spoon the honey
From the pot
I am alive.
I sip that potion.

"A Hymn From a Choir I Stopped Hearing"
- F. Doherty

Hear it?

Hear it?

Did I ever l listen?
Loving through deaths
Through betrayals
Could I hear?

Buried in debris

Splinters, soft hands
Massaging my body
Remnants of childhood
Dripping sounds
Life lived?
The choir…the music…
I know where it is. Need I say?

I Dunno

I dunno why I'm named
Regina
My parents called me
Rifka

And I marched on May Day
In the Jewish Section
Of the I.W.O.*
We despised the wealthy
Spoke Yiddish at home
Loved Klezmer music

I dunno why the kids on
our block called us
Christ killers
I dunno why I was told
Blondes are sexy and beautiful
When I never met a natural blonde

I dunno why we never heard
Bessie Smith in music appreciation class
Or Paul Robeson
I dunno why we mutter Thank God
When a cop pulls us over, doesn't shoot
Let's us go
Still speeding down a highway
I don't know why the stock market
Is bullish or bearish
Soft or hard
I just waited for my check
Under the name
Regina.

*I.W.O. was International Workers Order and was declared illegal by Senator McCarthy in 1956.

It Is What It Is

A personal story
I listen and hear
"It is what it is…"
Say phone pals
Sage advice
Freely given

Yesterday I counted
Cacophonous voices
Assuring me
It is what it is

Yes, I nod at the wall
Gaze at the garden weeds
Wear cheap suits
Sit in a plastic chair
Speechless, hurt perhaps
Does it matter?
Matter…at all.

Linen Jacket

The white, linen jacket
A hand me down
Lovely, crisp, free moving

I grabbed it whenever I was invited
For a drive to anywhere

I was six or maybe five
Loving to go away
Away from sadness
Pain, holocaust remembrance

Dead,--all gone—never to return
In the fire, frenzy of Europe
Somewhere

I recall
A rumble seat car
I was considered sweet, acceptable.
Invited,
I'd go anywhere
Anyway

Looks Younger

Looks younger

Would you believe it?
She's 53 and looks wonderful.
Ask Dr. Oz

No lines
No wrinkles
No sag
No age
No life
Beautiful, waxen doll
Uncomplaining
Silent
Submissive
We'll keep her
For awhile
Saleable for creams and smiles
Play toy...for now.

Moving On?

Yes…got to go
Where?
Night time where the clock
Has hands

I can go there
Part of world
Organization

Have to go
Got to go.

Darkness…privacy
One great mound of excrement
Fleeing before execution.

Noise

I do hear
The noises
Or is it simply
Noise

"It is insufferable…"
I am informed
Cacophony continues
I am busy

Dying
It is my full-time
Occupation
Can't entertain various, sundry
Needs of others

Right now
Perhaps never again…

Sorry, I'll call back
If…when…O.K?
To hear of pain, depression, anger
When I am able.

Nothingness

I have perfected
Activity?
Doing nothing
Legs on chair
Seated at kitchen table
Reading…
News of the day

Laundered, cleansed
I read anyway…
Silence
Phone, I command
Don't ring!

I must answer
Can't let it ring
One never knows
Can't be certain

I pursue mastering
Legs up
Employed in waiting

I sit in repose at Bedford Hills prison
Waiting?

I had melancholy thoughts
a strangeness in my mind,
A feeling that I was not for that hour,
Not for that place.
              - William Wordsworth, "The Prelude"

Not for That Place

It isn't the robin banging his body
Against the front room window

It isn't the narcissist I know
Who is very busy
Certainly she cannot speak to me
When I raise an issue about my needs
Even though she phoned me!

It isn't that mostly all attendees
At conferences on victims of
human sex trafficking
Are women

Men do attend when there are
Crimes against humanity
Women not humanity?

It isn't that I am terribly annoying,
Confrontational
When I discuss horrors in American prisons
Including rapes while in shackles
And torture in solitary 8 by 10 cells

It isn't conditions in leaking nuclear plants
Within a radius of suburban homes
and the huge population
In New York City

It isn't my pleas for conversation
Instead of

"How are you?"
"I am great."

I am definitely
Not of that place
Nor of this place
I recognize the fixed face
The golden glow of yellow hair
Sparkling eye lashes

Am I in a prelude to a main event
And a potential climax?

Should I hide?
Kick an old can down the road?
Wear more purple
Say "no" more often?

Should I, can I, may I
Think it
Do it
Love it
Wallow in it
Recall it?

I emerge from the tunnel
View the grey sky
It is…I guess
I know
It is!

On Life
to Ernest Hemingway

The divisions of periods
In eras and decades
Arbitrary
Fashion designers set standards

The novel, like life,
Transcends style
At the center of the frantic search
For answers
As the last platoon
Seeks to seize the moment
Each of us moves
Along a clogged path
Avoiding debris and traps

On our daily rounds
Aching, surviving
Life is truth?
Waiting for sound
In greeting.

We live in this time
In this place
Bang into barriers
To reach
Beyond the shadows
To a well lighted room.

Paper and Pens

Soft velvet pens
Uniball gift
"Write," a voice intoned

Moving across lovely paper
Signal - love
Pens are soft, clear, bright
Without delusions
Detritus, denial
Deceit

I place words on computer
Love - still true

Parts of Me

Parts of me
Those parts they'd never see
Or maybe they did
The lost, lonely child
Grabbing her linen jacket
Running from the cramped apartment
Going driving
With anyone riding away

The need was excessive
The selfish fear dominated her long life
She was never in the "here"
She was going away
Away
Never losing the need for love
For the round, small child
Who sucked her thumb
In the corner
Away
Was not unusual
Or very smart
Or very pretty
Or very talented
Or very...

She settled in
Grew old
Colored her hair
Pierced her ears
Wore silly clothes
All the same
Inside,
All the same.

Preoccupied/Occupied

Warm,
Hand shakes
Occupied
"Sorry, I'm busy
Very hectic life
Get together
Of course,
Soon"

Occupied
In the Square
Near Wall Street
Inside warm,
Hand shakes
Investment bankers
Investing our lives
Their desires, plans, goals

I remain
Preoccupied
Harried, anxious
Drone droppings
Good cheer
Or extermination.

Penny

I am finally telling it like it is! Never cry, act tough and don't fool with me. I've been here in Bedford since 1981, and before that I was upstate in medium security. What does everyone say in group programs? Counting the days to go home. What a crock... Sounds good. It isn't true. I have no idea of what's up in the outside world. Never worked, never drove a car, never had a personal life. Never shopped for food or raised kids or had sex with a man. So much more. Never made any decisions. Choices? What's that? It is just a word because I have no choices in here.

I've battled my demons and now I'm 55. I do admire Obama. But, honestly, I never voted and I wouldn't be allowed to.

I know what I do well. I am an excellent porter and when I wash the floors, the tiles are clean. The water in the pail is clear. I've been doing it for years and everyone knows Penny can get the cell block shining in 3 to 4 hours.

I used to fight over everything. You better watch your back and your front was the word for years. Only one thing triggers my anger now and that's my breast cancer and mastectomy. This bitch said to me last week, "I guess your breasts are chopped off now?" I nearly knocked her teeth in, but my friend, Donna, held me in a warm hug. My heart was beating real fast.

I know I can write some good poems and I do write for some women here who have young kids.

So I'm going to level with this group. I don't want to leave here; you are my family and that's for my lifetime. If I leave I won't see you again and that makes me want to cry. What's out there? Struggle and pain and that's what got me here in the first place. It sounds nuts so no one talks about it. I am nuts and on three different drugs to control my emotions.

I've seen people come and go and come back again. Some of us have been together for a long time. I've grown in here and my days are numbered. Just completed a round of chemo and radiation and my friends brought me broth when I couldn't raise my head. I am known in here and I know who to count on. I am scared and I cry now. Outside I'd be an old house cleaner. In here I am Penny, not to be played with. What can I do? No one laughs at me here.

Remember Tom Paine

Funny, fat guy
Unkempt, muttering
Stumbling, stuttering
Tom Paine
He wrote tracts
I recall his words
My childhood.

Forty children
Second grade
"Yes, children,
Sister will take
Catholic children for
Religious instruction."

I sat alone
In front row
Small, nervous
Weepy inside

I did not know.
Religious instruction?
"Poppa," I asked at midnight
Store was closed.

"It is an a apothecary,
Not a store."
Mama said
Whatever it was
Poppa was exhausted
Grey, tense, thin

"Poppa, I can't sleep
I love you, Poppa
Why don't I have religious
instruction?"

"Mamele, remember
You are religious.
It is in our actions
I will give you Tom Paine's book."
Poppa was exhausted

Rip the Bodies

Dot Com
Dot.Dot
Come here

Love, Faith, Prey
Prey on children
Values...Lives
Come here
Learn your ABC's
Pass your GED's
Your SAT's
Your...what is it?
In God We Trust
We are patriotic
Our truth will prevail
Bombs bursting, yes
Drones will swoop down
Black as herons
Collateral damage unavoidable
Women find shelter

Robin

Robin bangs
My window
His body blows
Are incomprehensible
To me, a human

How can I learn from robin
To bang against the power
Of bureaucratic "no"?

Free myself
From anger, frustration, lassitude

The robin flies away
When I approach
The window

Does he want to come inside?
I leave the room
His banging against glass
Continues…

The rhythm is precise
Bang, bang, bang, bang
Until I return

How long can robin and I
Play hide and seek
Role sharing?

The powerful glass will not yield
To robin's small body
I must disappear.

Shards of Glass

Shards of glass…moments of anger
I grasp…weakly, uncertainly
The body I still possess
I walk, chat, question
Dangerously moving my arms
In the air

Not as ballerina
But blind and ancient
Sounds in my head recall
"Yes, I am somebody!"
Who?
Not a Moslem woman
Sheathed in shawls, scarves and
False modesty.
Not a fashion icon
Teasing the photo shot with flabby cleavage
Just a breathing, searching
Bent woman
With a dim lamp
Devoted to finding
That answer to an ancient question.

Space and Time

We live in space and time
We nurture ourselves
Wear spandex or extra large
We lick the asses of the rich
Or casual tribes of formulaic
Beauty
Cleavage?
Blonde washed-out wigs
Worn botox skin

We still die
Have casual sex
Reproduce
Switch and return
We still die.

Something That Never Was

In the time of your life…
A phrase I recall from childhood
Said by a known writer
No longer read

But we are here
In the time of our lives
Moving about
Wondering why paintings hang on walls
In museums?

Why babies are wheeled
In carriages with wheels?
Why people eat three times a day
Why hair is colored, curled, twisted,
Into shapes.

Why women carry bags called pocket books
Or purses.
Why men walk freer?
Why girls wear dresses
Long and short
Always years ago
Why styles are set
By people we never met
Why being quiet was
Learned in school.

Why stamps are placed
On envelopes
Why computers hold our records
Why we try to feel less lonely.
Can we ever succeed?

The Open Road?

Waiting for gas pump
To ride on Whitman's open road
Or clogged highway
The road beckons
Not me

Mental prison
Control and deceit
Poisoned rivers and soon oceans
Nuclear fallout
Waiting are coffee plantations.
Tranquility?

The road not explored.

"The past is the present, isn't it? It's the future, too. We all try to lie out of that, but life won't let us."
  - Mary Tyrone, *Long Day's Journey Into Night*, Eugene O'Neill

The Past Is the Present Is the Future

Am I listening to my own voice? Who am I responding to? Do we simply curse the Man? Rikers Island prison school in a dirty trailer does not reflect the bleak life for these young men. Who the hell do I think I am? The guys frequently fall asleep on the desks or stare into space. Are they thinking about the girlfriends and babies they left behind? While the kids grow and develop they rot in prison.

Can I reach any of them? Do the CO's serve as correction counselors or even hearers at the school? Can they read and write? Is it all a scam? So what is a prison? Eager reformers or despotic servants of the State have claims about who is responsible for the lives beyond the walls and bars and gates and electrified fences, barbed wire and shackle chairs. Who wonders, who cares who wears college rings or joins a frat? You can't fight City Hall and who goes to Harvard. Argue, cajole, get in, get out. The rule of the land is…There ought to be a law. We do know we are powerless so what's the response?

Prison…a life away, an animal existence. A cure? What a farce, she thinks as she climbs the metal stairs armed with poetry and pencils. These people in prison are stuffed away with endless "free" time. Is she free? Guilty of pretense, getting to "know who I am." She never learned how to be beautiful, wear makeup, mix drinks, wear nail polish, blow dry hair, is confused about setting a lovely table, folding napkins, voting for the right candidate based on party politics, be acceptable. Can you be a wedding planner, a net worker, a captain of industry, a who?

A searcher for cobwebs, a keeper of the keys, a proper adult. Yes… that's it. Stay ready to leave the lock up at any moment.

The Shower

Showers have many images for me…
People die in showers, sing in showers
Magnificent sound
I create poems in my mind
Head, I mean?
Body?

They are sad
Or cynical
I conceal the ache and fear
Of obliteration
Meaning less?
The sound of one hand clapping
Face to face contact
With eyeless faces
Waiting for Godot
Or my father?
No identity
Somewhere in a place like Prague
Dark, dank, alien
Can this be shower writing?
Words disappear as I write.

"There is no sun without a shadow, and it is essential to know the night"
- Albert Camus, The Myth of Sisyphus

The Sun and It's Shadow

She recalls wanting to kill executioners. Victim strapped to a gurney lying down. The warden, the tie down team, corrections team - all employed in a death industry - legal and sanctioned by the government.

Cages to lock up the discarded, the desperate, the disabled, the psychotic. Investment in one Texas Ranger shortstop - 250 million over a 10-year contract.

Jails are great business.

Living children drinking dangerous water...eating lead paint... fathers in prison...called super-predators. Nicky writes from prison... "I see emptiness. No money for courses here. Where can we go after years in cages? No use to no one...Don't send books without permission. They'll be thrown away or confiscated. Send stuff from stores on official list. Business, you know. Only four more years...Sending love. That's a joke. Take care."

To Bill

The world, my world stops
On this day
Yearly

Significant
Momentous occasion?
End of all wars?
Love conquers all
Especially evil.

The ground hogs
In Shakespeare's theater
Will chew their nuts
First perusing the environment
The world.

Today is simply
The birthday
Of my life's love.

To Robin

Robin you win!
Bang as you desire
Unstoppable...Defiant

Delicate robin
You are steel
I submit, broken
Defeated.

Take on the house
The trees, the lawn,
The flowering willow

Bang on my window
I cannot invite you in!

We Are Good...We Are!

Do we simply sign petitions?
Raise our arms and sway
Peace, Love, Hope, Generosity

Do we?
Salute ourselves
We are good, caring, loving
We smile at gas stations

No stranger met without a hug
No longer kiss babies
Even when we're losing
We're juicing nourishment

Plenty of orange and color
Purple, deep red
We love ourselves
Accept our ignorance
But?
We are.

"I wake to sleep, and take my waking slow"
- Emily Dickinson

We Take Our Waking Slow

Submission?
Aggression?
Pretense?

Seize the moment
A spirit response
Moving in a supine posture...

Crawling
To seek sustenance
A community
Cacophonous, clanging, banging
Sounds that make no sense at all.

So...why bother?
Why try to explain?
It is inexplicable
Because it is.

Lights across the bay
Winter Dreams*
"Up" elevator
On "down" button

Alice through the distorted mirror
Broken glass
Choices?
Indecision?
Endless...

Primo Levi
Remember
Only the dead survive
The living perish in fiery ovens
Ash and sand
Remember!

We Exist

We do exist between a sleep
And awakening, a death
We speed, march forward
Why? Do not recall
Search for ashes
Search for reasons
Must do… wake up…
Must move… where?

The airy home
The breezy road
The long sought dream
The wish fulfilled
The colors blend
Life is a carousel
Round and round
Bloated with hope
Waiting for the leader
Who waits for us.

Yes

Staring at...nothing

I saw old women
Seated in the sun
Outside buildings
Hardly moving
Seeming in thought

I never wondered
About their psyches
Threads of still life
Ending those final days
In chairs
Some with wheels
Blankets covering withered legs

Did they love, hate, care
question, beg,or sleep soundly
Dreaming of a future
Or oblivion?
I noted their coiffed
Blonde hair
Polished nails
Did it please them?

I sit at the kitchen table
As my mother sat
Blank, immobile
Not able to break the spell
I rise, pour coffee
It stands
Solitary and cold.

The Best Way to Think About Reality Is To Get As
Far Away From it as Possible.
                    - Haruki Murakami, *Kafka on the Shore*

Meaning

Meaning
Is significant...
Did I lose it?
Meaning about...?
Actors strutting their wares for us
To make millions?
Purchase, possess
As we pant in the corner
Richard Cory's
Disciples?

I read - avidly - for meaning
The Star, The Enquirer
View puffed up lips
Bouncing breasts peeking over tight bodices
Murders
From California or Arizona suburbs.

Meaning slipping away
Eros or Enron
High School as bizarre
Experience for successful American kids?

Poison in Tokyo subways
Soldiers bringing freedom
To starving or nearly dead children?
Some limbless, numbed
By betrayal
Sustained by hate
Young born old
Hell?

Psychoanalytic trained guru says
"Better late than never."

We'll meet
Kafka near Tiffany's
"Penny wise pound foolish
"A stitch in time saves nine."
Smiling malevolently
Keep hand on a
Diamond knife.

Meaning must be
In diet Pepsi
New Balance shoes
Timberland boots
Glen Gould at the piano.

Incarceration as rehabilitation?

Colonel Sanders as Henry VIII
Chomping on succulent bones
Or Jonathan Swift's babies
Victims of famine?

Is it Red Label or Black
Straight, no ice cubes
Meaning as gargle
Loneliness?

Clothes, fashion, drugs, ephemera
Baseball cap on backwards
Meaning to be found
In the next scheduled event?

To Yetta

I have carried
Yetta like a hidden jewel
Between my toes
Smooth, shiny
A small sliver of hope
For future and past
My mother's name
Survivor of a cramped ghetto life.

Yetta, first grand child
Of my life
Dancing beyond the reach
Of turbulent waves
Diving into the ocean fluid
Coming up in bright expectation
Of taste of life
To yet unknown world.

About the Author

The author, Regina (Rifka) Krummel received her Ed.D from Columbia's Teachers' College, taught at NYU, Columbia and many other universities and schools. She retired from Queens College CUNY, after 33 years, as Full Professor, Emerita. She has spent many years doing poetry therapy and creative writing in prisons in the UK and USA. She trained future high school teachers at Rikers Island's male prison. She did poetry therapy in the New York State women's maximum security prison in the psychiatric division of the institution. She continues to teach creative writing in an adult program in Connecticut. Together with her husband Dr. William Krummel, she has volunteered in India and China in the area of education and professional development for teachers of English. She believes living is an endless search in expanding one's knowledge of the world through teaching and exploring new cultures, including the dehumanizing effects of the whitewashed American prison system.

Krummel's standards in her own poetry are reflected in the standards she set for students in her classes. Students had the following comments about the effect she had on their writing and their lives:

"I e-mailed Regina a piece I had written about my wife and fly fishing. "Please look this over and tell me what you think." I received a two sentence response telling me that my story was "in the last sentence. Get rid of this fishing stuff and start there." That was nothing if not direct. And correct. She demanded introspection, honesty, and passion in my writing. She taught me how to embrace the power of words. She insisted on that."

-Frank Doherty

"[Upon meeting Professor Krummel as an undergraduate] I was impressed with her openness, and graciousness. She spoke of her commitment to education, social activism and literacy as the vehicles for unraveling the truth hidden in both light and dark shadows. I instantly admired her no-nonsense manner of articulation that lacked any superficiality or pretense and her deep respect and intellectual drive to search for and give meaning to life. Professor Krummel's social activism and lifelong work teaching incarcerated men and women deeply inspired me. Upon my graduation from college she helped me get my first assignment at Riker's Island Correctional Facility in the Rose M. Singer building teaching English to incarcerated women that lasted for several years of my life."

-Michelle Redman

"Regina's wisdom, sensitivity and brilliant sense of humor helped students across the spectrum to come to the realization that teaching and learning is not repetition or retrieval, nor acquisition of skills nor cramming for examinations. Students learned that each of us has the ability to consciously introspect and reflect upon our own lives and the lives and experiences of others to produce original and significant prose and poetry."

- Bert Honigman, Long Island Middle School Principal (ret.)

"Ultimately rendering our experiences, our coping in this world, and translating the often-paradoxical moods of the human beast, to paper in the simplest, most relatable light, is why we take writing classes after work. Regina Krummel does this superbly in her writing.

- Manuel Allende, Student, Creative Writing,
Norwalk Community College

More praise for *On The Ledge*

"Regina Krummel has a powerful poetic voice. She reflects the inner thoughts of prison inmates, as illustrated in her poem: "And the Gates Clang Shut"; while her poem "Desultory" describes her current thoughts and fears. As a physician, I can see that she embodies the fear of cancer in the latter poem. She is also able to relay the fears of other cancer sufferers described in her narrative, "Penny." Dr. Krummel's avant garde ideas expressed in her writing, fashions the way that she crafts poetry and her narratives. Despite the dark themes that are a part of life, she is also able to reflect the beauty and joie de vivre of her grand-children, as illustrated in her poem "To Yetta.""

- Soma Sengupta, MD, Ph.D.
Published poet and physician-scientist at Emory University

"There is no hiding in Regina's poems. The emotions of the moment are completely experienced by the reader. Her lucid descriptions of childhood memories as well as current circumstances are all there to ponder. I always feel like I understand where she is coming from and that is her gift."

- Richard Krivo, Senior Principal Data Scientist at Symantec

www.ingramcontent.com/pod-product-compliance
Lightning Source LLC
Chambersburg PA
CBHW060714030426
42337CB00017B/2873